A FIRST LOOK AT CATS

By Millicent E. Selsam and Joyce Hunt

ILLUSTRATED BY HARRIETT SPRINGER

WALKER AND COMPANY ☀ **NEW YORK**

Library of Congress Cataloging in Publication Data

Selsam, Millicent Ellis, 1912–
  A first look at cats.

  (A First look at series)
  SUMMARY: A brief introduction to the physical
characteristics, habits, and natural environment of
various members of the cat family.
  1. Felidae—Juvenile literature. 2. Cats—Juvenile
literature. [1. Cats. 2. Felidae]
I. Hunt, Joyce, joint author. II. Springer,
Harriett. III. Title.
QL737.C23S44   1981   599.74′428   80-7673
ISBN 0-8027-6398-7
ISBN 0-8027-6399-5 (lib. bdg.)

Text copyright © 1981 by Millicent E. Selsam and
Joyce Hunt
Illustrations copyright © 1981 by Harriett Springer

First published in the United States of America in 1981
by the Walker Publishing Company, Inc.

Published simultaneously in Canada by Beaverbooks,
Limited, Pickering, Ontario.

Trade ISBN: 0-8027-6398-7
Reinf. ISBN: 0-8027-6399-5
Library of Congress Catalog Card Number: 80-7673

Printed in the United States of America

10 9 8 7 6 5 4 3 2 1

A *FIRST LOOK AT* SERIES

Each of the nature books for this series is planned to develop the child's powers of observation and give him or her a rudimentary grasp of scientific classification.

For Carolyn

The authors wish to thank Dr. Richard Van Gelder, a curator in the American Museum of Natural History, for reading the text of this book.

Here is a cat.

Here is another cat.

What makes a cat a cat?

A cat is a mammal because it has hair
and its babies nurse on the mother's milk.

Cats belong to a group of mammals called *Carnivora* (Kar-*niv*-aw-rah).

Most carnivores (*kar*-ni-vawrs) have powerful jaws and sharp, pointed teeth which help them to catch animals and tear their flesh.

Dogs, wolves, and foxes are also carnivores.

DOG

WOLF

FOX

But cats are different from all other carnivores.
Their sharp claws are more curved and can be pulled back
into their paws.
Their tongues are rough because they are covered
with tiny sharp points.
Most cats roar or meow.

CLAWS OUT

CLAWS IN

TONGUE

How do you tell cats apart?
There are big cats that can roar.

JAGUAR

TIGER

LION

There are small cats that cannot roar.
They meow and purr.
One kind of small cat that meows and purrs
is our house cat.

OCELOT

HOUSE CAT

SERVAL

11

There is also one kind of cat, the cheetah,
that does not roar, meow, or purr.
Sometimes it chirps like a bird.
Sometimes it barks like a dog.

CHEETAH

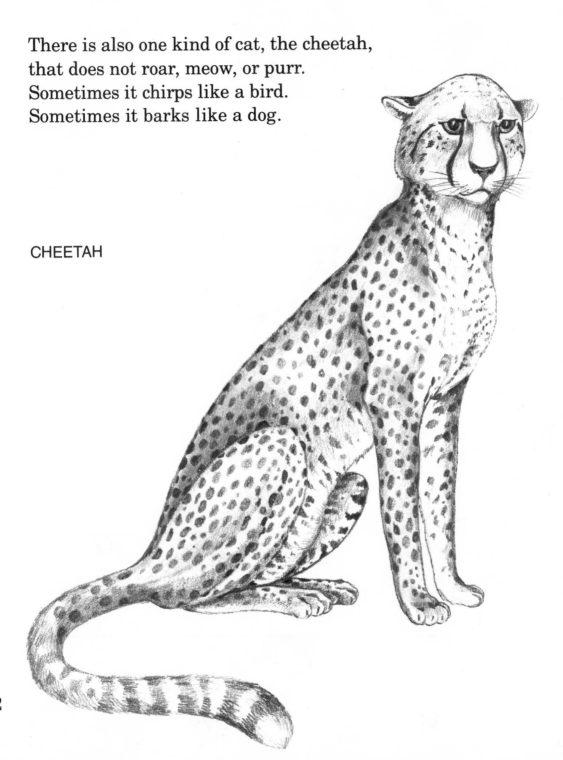

12

BIG CATS THAT ROAR

How do you tell one big cat from another?
Nobody has to tell you the difference
between a *lion* and a *tiger*.

ONLY THE MALE LION HAS A MANE.

But it is harder to tell the difference
between a *jaguar* and a *leopard*.

They both have spots in small circles called *rosettes*.
But only the jaguar has a dark spot
in the center of its rosettes.

JAGUAR ROSETTES

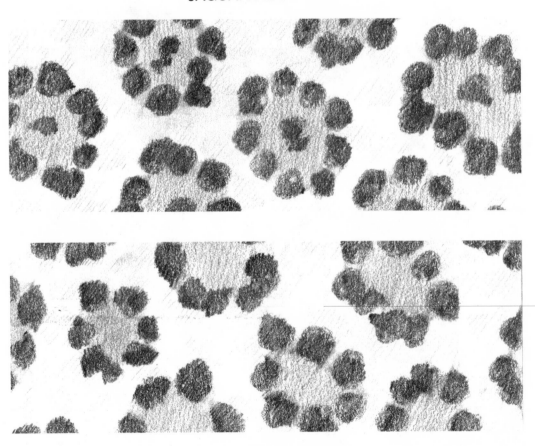

LEOPARD ROSETTES

Which is the jaguar?
Which is the leopard?

Some leopards are all black. They are called *black panthers*.

15

SMALL CATS THAT MEOW AND PURR

How do you tell one small cat from another?
Sometimes the markings help.
Many small cats have stripes, spots, or blotches.
Find the cat with two dark stripes down each cheek.
Find the cat with dark stripes around its legs.

SAND CAT

PALLAS CAT

Notice the ears.
They stick out on each side of the flat heads.

16

These two cats have short tails.
Look at the markings at the tips of their tails.
Find the tail tip that is black all around.
Find the tail tip that is black only on top.

BOBCAT

LYNX

Notice <u>these</u> ears.
They are pointed and have hairs growing from the tips.
Also look at their side-whiskers.

The markings and the ears help tell these cats apart, too.
Look for the spotted cat.
Look for the cat with no spots.
Which cat has very large round ears?
Which cat has very large pointed ears?

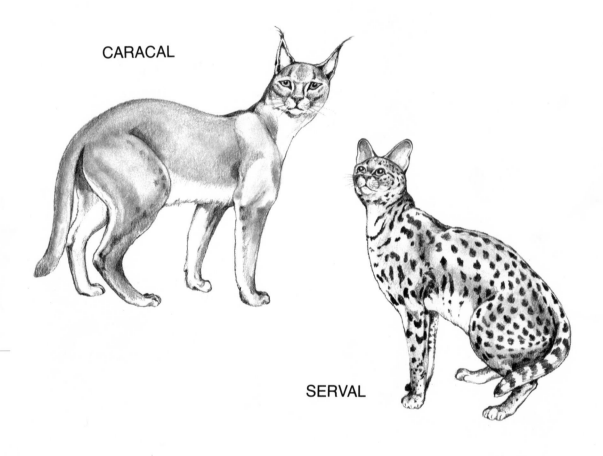

CARACAL

SERVAL

18

Sometimes size is a clue.
Here are two spotted cats.
Their markings are almost the same.
But the *margay* is smaller than the *ocelot*.

Size also helps to tell the difference
between these two cats.
Both have large blotches on their fur.
The smaller cat is a *marbled cat*.
The larger one is a *clouded leopard*.

There are no markings on the bodies of these two cats.
Both are long and narrow.
But the *jaguarundi* (jag-war-*un*-dee) is
much smaller than the *mountain lion* and has much
shorter legs.

The mountain lion is also called a cougar,
a panther, or a puma.

CHEETAH

The cheetah is in a group by itself because
it does not roar or meow (see page 12). Also, its claws
cannot be pulled all the way back into its paws.
Look for the black line that runs
from the corner of its eye to its lip.
This spotted cat has very long legs that help it
to run short distances at a speed of
more than 70 miles (110 kilometers) an hour.

This is an *African wildcat*.
More than three thousand years ago in the land of Egypt
this small cat was used to kill mice.
Many scientists think that these African cats
were the ancestors of our house cats.

HOUSE CATS

Here are two kinds of house cats:
long-haired and short-haired.

25

LONG-HAIRED CATS

These cats come in many colors.
Match the cats to their names.

BLACK PERSIAN
WHITE PERSIAN
TABBY (striped)
CALICO (patches of color)

SHORT-HAIRED CATS

Which cat has wavy hair?
Which cat has dark feet and a dark face and tail?

REX

SIAMESE

28

MANX

What's missing on this cat?

TO TELL WILD CATS APART:

Look at the size.

Look at the markings.

Look at the ears.

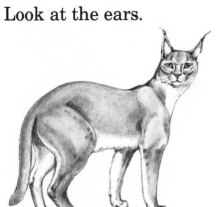

TO TELL HOUSE CATS APART:

Look for long or short hair.

Look at the markings.